The Desiderata
of Love

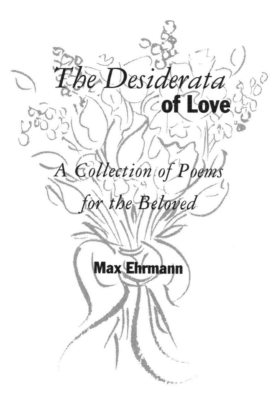

The Desiderata
of Love

A Collection of Poems
for the Beloved

Max Ehrmann

Crown Publishers, Inc.
New York

Published by Crown Publishers, Inc., 201 East 50th Street,
New York, New York 10022.
Member of the Crown Publishing Group.
Random House, Inc. New York, Toronto, London, Sydney, Auckland
CROWN is a trademark of Crown Publishers, Inc.

Manufactured in the United States of America

Library of Congress Cataloging-in-Publication Data
Ehrmann, Max, 1872–1945.
The desiderata of love : a collection of poems for the beloved /
Max Ehrmann. — 1st ed.
1. Love poetry, American. I. Title.
PS3509.H7D44 1995
811′.52—dc20   94–43824

Illustrations by Sally Sturman

Book design by Linda Kocur

ISBN 0-517-70078-6
10 9 8 7 6 5 4 3 2 1
First Crown Publishers Edition

contents

introduction

Max Ehrmann had been known only as the author of the timeless *Desiderata*. That is a great achievement, but recognition of his previously unknown abilities has been spreading with the publication in 1992 of *The Desiderata of Happiness*. Now with *The Desiderata of Love: A Collection of Poems for the Beloved*, he emerges as a poet of depth and sensitivity in the greatest of mankind's wants.

We have only a short time to care for those to whom we are bound by ties of love. Do not hesitate. Seize the moment. The most important memories in our lives involve relationships of love and sentiment.

So it is no surprise that newspapers and magazines expend considerable money and space on writing of love problems and happenings. In fact, *Bartlett's Quotations* devotes nineteen columns to love—the largest section in the book. (War only gets six.)

You will do far more than merely enjoy this book. You will relate to it. Enjoy your memories, and anticipate those to come.

Robert L. Bell

The Desiderata
of Love

desiderata

Go placidly amid the noise and the haste, and
remember what peace there may be in silence.
As far as possible, without surrender, be on good
terms with all persons. Speak your truth quietly and
clearly; and listen to others, even to the dull and
ignorant; they too have their story. Avoid loud
and aggressive persons; they are vexatious to the
spirit. If you compare yourself with others, you
may become vain or bitter, for always there will be
greater and lesser persons than yourself. Enjoy
your achievements as well as your plans. Keep
interested in your own career, however humble; it is
a real possession in the changing fortunes of time.

Exercise caution in your business affairs, for the world is full of trickery. But let this not blind you to what virtue there is; many persons strive for high ideals, and everywhere life is full of heroism. Be yourself. Especially do not feign affection. Neither be cynical about love; for in the face of all aridity and disenchantment, it is as perennial as the grass. Take kindly the counsel of the years, gracefully surrendering the things of youth. Nurture strength of spirit to shield you in sudden misfortune. But do not distress yourself with dark imaginings. Many fears are born of fatigue and loneliness. Beyond a wholesome discipline, be gentle with yourself. You are a child of the universe no less than the trees and the stars; you have a right to be here. And whether or not it is clear to you, no doubt the universe is unfolding as it should.

Therefore be at peace with God, whatever you conceive Him to be. And whatever your labors and aspirations, in the noisy confusion of life, keep peace in your soul. With all its sham, drudgery and broken dreams, it is still a beautiful world. Be cheerful. Strive to be happy.

how beautiful **is life!**

"How beautiful is life!" he thought.

They were waltzing to the "Blue Danube."

She was fragrant with rose leaves and lilies of the
    valley, her cheek pressed to his.

"How beautiful is life!"

He knew she was good as well as beautiful. And she
    had another fragrance: that of the clean, young,
    healthy human-angel.

"Ah, to feel like this always! To go to the journey's
    end, like this, with her! How beautiful is life!"

Then twenty-eight years of hard, anxious work,
    until he died, to pay for this night of dream.

only
the loved

I dreamed last night that I lay in the ground,
But was not dead. There was no sound or sight;
Yet I could think; and waited as one bound
For God to cut the cords and let in light.

Time passed. O time hangs heavy in the grave;
It is a stony land where naught will grow,
A surgeless sea whose waters will not wave—
Waiting for God within my bed of woe.

Then whispers came. I heard the people talk,
As they looked on the grass that grew o'er me;
And each one measured up my daily walk.
None praised. The Vulgar with my name made free.

Is God asleep? Then came a woman's sobs.
Such sobs that made me break my earthen den.
As I came forth, I heard God say, "Love robs
The grave; only the loved shall live again."

to be **loved**

To be loved in life is life's greatest gift.

To be loved in death for some bit of beauty one has given the world, is to take from death some of its sting.

Life has need of all the charm of word and sound, of color and carven stone that love can give it.

a man
and a woman

A man and a woman once walked in the evening
to a wood, that the trees might hide them from
the light.

Far into the deep shadows wandered they, when one
said, in fear, "Let us return." It does not matter
which one said it.

Still they wandered in the dark, watching the light
within themselves, as it glowed in the garden of
their love.

The night came over the world and the wood; and
seeing they had tarried too long, they determined
to return at dawn.

But—it is an odd story—do you know, it never
again grew morning in that wood?

when i
come home

When I come home will you be there to greet
Me with a smile and outstretched arms,
A heart of quickened beat,
When our eyes meet?

And will you tell me all your thoughts and deeds,
As in the gloaming night again
We take the path that leads
O'er grassy meads?

And as of old will you my grief beguile—
The grief the weary days have brought?
And will you make me smile
With you the while?

And as the mellow years come on, will you
Remember still that love is young
And fresh as morning dew
For me and you?

I'm coming home ere long to you who wait
So patiently as seasons go,
Beside the woodland gate
In evenings late.

In fancy's eye a thousand times I see
You there with eager, anxious look
That scans the rolling lea
In search of me.

I see you run into my arms at last,
And feel the tremor of your lips.
The world aside is cast,
And care is past.

I'm coming home ere long to you who wait
So patiently as seasons go,
Beside the woodland gate
In evenings late.

the one
woman

How could I help but love you, coming up a cool
and radiant fountain in the hot and dreary night
of life?
I swear the sins of youthful women lay upon my
hands, the grimy sweat of wearied men in strife,
Who'd clothed my body with garments fair, and the
agonies of children, too, condemned to toil that I
might freely live.
I swear the cries of beaten slaves turned not my ear,
nor wails of stunted children that the sea of want
doth give.
There was no order in my days. I slept and ate as
instinct called, and heeded every wanton passion
near,
A face, a form, a game of chance, the gossip of the
idle wags, and lived to finish quickly earth's career.

And though I shall regret what now I here confess,
and cringing turn from this swift lash that o'er my
back I send—
I swear that thing called soul had not set torch
within the bloodstained walls where creaked my
heart, bent on low passion's end.
How could I help but love you, coming like a
balmy light into the dead and moonless night of
empty years?
You spoke, and I saw the blood of murdered
innocence glare red upon my hands, and heard
the wailing sea of tears.
You touched my hand, and through my restless life
stole scenes of quiet woods and dancing shafts of
gold upon the green;
And daffodils and running vines, and larks' and
linnets' songs, and the softly sounding lyre of doves
perched high unseen.
Things I had dreamed of in my dreaming childhood
came again, and solitude with you was what I longed
for most;

Out of other distant worlds remembered visions
sprang that long ere earthly birth I knew 'mid
God's immortal host.

And when I kissed your lips this world was born
again, and in the still and starry night I was with
you and God;

And truth and mercy bloomed within my soul, and
kindly words bred fast upon my lips, and bliss came
where I trod.

And long I lay upon the grassy earth, your hand in
mine, and listened to your voice that showed the
better way;

And your own God I learned to love, but loved you
more o'er all I ever knew, you who were fated not
to stay.

If I am aught, and tired men and weary women
know my voice, and smile amid their tears, it is
for you;

And if a song has left my lips, some clear and
simple song that comfort brings within some lonely
heart of rue,

It is not mine, but comes from out the mellow
shaded woods of memory now mouldering in the
faded past;
And if the springtide and the autumn bring reborn
the songs of love, it is because your spirit holds me
fast—
Because I pressed my lips to yours in the secret,
voiceless woods, where daffodils and running vines
forever blow;
And where in tender dreams of waking hours,
through all the silent years, my vagrant footsteps
often come and go.

the one
man

The written law and the custom had denied me
love. But as with other women, instinct had taught
me to be silent. I was in the flower of my youth,
and each day I hungered more and more.

Still, when I uttered a sound, the elders raised their
fingers, and shamed me to silence, saying that love
was only according to the written law and the
custom.

Thus a year passed, and several years passed, and the
flower of my youth began to fade, and the eternal
hunger in my heart made me sick of soul, and joy
was no more in me.

Then one night I lifted my eyes again to the god of my childhood, and again earnestly I sought an answer in the stars; when lo! I saw that the written law and the custom were man-made, and that the hunger in my heart and the flower of my youth were God-made.

And I trod forth in the middle of the night to yield myself to the arms that would hold me fast, and to the lips that would moisten mine. And my heart beat as never before, and the stars sang, and the night and the god of the night smiled upon me.

And when I came to the arms that would hold me fast and the lips that would moisten mine to give myself up, I said, "Here, pluck the flower of my youth, and feed my heart."

But the arms of him I loved were listless and would entwine me not, nor would his lips press mine; and there was some talk, and I cried aloud bitterly, understanding not. Then said he I loved, "The written law and the custom would crucify you on the street before all the people."

I went away, and walked in the dim night, wondering why the people should deny the will of God, and punish them that obey His command, for the love in me was heaven-born.

And soon thereafter I returned to him I loved, and said, "I will endure the punishment of the written law and the custom, touch me, touch me, touch me with your hand! and I will proclaim my joy aloud; for what is wrought in love's name is justified of God."

"Then," said he, "must you perish, for they that need the written law and the custom will not hold them guiltless that need it not."

"Death be welcome," I cried, "better a thousand times to live an hour and love and die at once, in the night, or be stoned upon the street, than die by inches, to wither and rot, and grow into old age as some unwatered flowerless vine, creeping over the juiceless earth, ugly to behold and barren."

"Wait," palliated my love, "perhaps all shall be fulfilled even yet according to the written law and the custom. Wait!"

"Waited have I all these years. The fruit is ripe, the time is here, it is the season. See, I am still beautiful, the rose still lights my cheek, my eyes not yet are dim, my bosom breathes like wind-swept fields of grain, and I nightly dream the dream of women loved!"

Then he said, "The written law and the custom are for the good of all the people, and the good of all the people is the will of God. Wait!"

"No," I cried, "I will have my hand touched by you whom I love. I will walk with you in the evening and in the night unafraid, and I will not part from you; the dawn shall be a knell for twain in your house, and the dusk shall not divide us."

"Wait!" said he again.

"I will tear down the walls that surround me, break the locks that imprison me, pull back the veil that blinds me. A mountain of laws shall not deny me, nor a sea of ice freeze my desire. I was made to breathe the sweet, and though death steal upon me at dusk, this day shall I follow the voice of the stars and the god of the stars."

Softly he said, "Too much I love you"; and touching me with his hand, he led me to where the day was darkening; and long we sat and spake no word, for the tumult was not of human speech; and soon the night came and the stars crept through the dark; yet spake he no word, nor touched me again with his hand.

And after a long time, in perfect calm, he whispered, "We will obey the law"; and arising, we wandered slowly off together, out into the light and the world.

yes

or no

(Suggested by the painting of Sir John Millais.)

I know my heart and yet I answer not,
For some I've seen grow sad by deep regret.
Better than love that fails is solitude,
Barren and hungry-hearted to the last.
It has still the happiness of day dreams,
For love that fails awakes the sleeper quick
With ruthless hands of saddened memory.
Better is solitude that still is sweet
In thought and not unkindly looked upon,
Whose virgin cheeks remember not love's kiss
At break of dawn nor in night's deepest sleep,
Whose breast is strange to touch of children's lips.
Far better not to know love's throbbing joy,
Than sadly to remember love is dead,

And hear cold words that once were soft and sweet,
And feel no more the press of eager arms
Where oft thy head did lie in bliss at eve,
And deign to beg where once thou didst permit.
Give me stern love that's fierce in jealousy,
Ardent, like love that's born by open fields
In silence save the soft winds whispering,
And grows each starry night by garden stile,
And lingers late before the last farewell;
So strange and wondrous sweet it would not part
But for the swiftly moving pallid stars
That call ere long the noiseless break of dawn;
Love that does not forget the first sweet kiss,
The gentle, hesitating touch of hand,
That blissful calm that made us one at first
By cheerful glow of winter evening fire;
Such love that stronger grows through changing
     years,
When age shall steal the rose from off my cheek
And dim my eyes and bend me slowly down.

And in that distant time wilt thou forget
The ancient trees 'neath which we sat at dusk,
And how, like twilight's spreading dark, our souls
Went forth with night's still music o'er the world,
And we both dwelt again in olden times
By glistening shores of sun-kissed golden seas,
And heard the echoed songs of all the world
Resound as softer grew the thickening dark?
Love's music old, wilt thou then break the reed
In twain by cruel neglect of thy warm lips?
Or wilt thou find the music sweeter still,
Like early childhood's oft-repeated songs?
Though I pale before thee on life's long way,
Wilt thou then still find joy in all my smiles?
And sit with gladness by my side at eve?
And walk with me through memory's olden lanes,
To mark again the hallowed spots where first
Thou kissed my cheek and shyly spoke my name—
Where once with saddened hearts we quarreled
    a while,

And thou with moistened eyes besought my love,
Which was again thine own ere thou didst ask—
And where in shade of yonder sighing woods
Oft tranced I sat and listened to thy hopes,
And silently implored a part in all
Close by thy side through joyous coming years?
When once I give thee all wilt thou forget,
In stress of other things, to kiss the lips
That yearn for thee by lonely evening light?
Then wilt thou whisper in my ear as now,
And set astir the chords of love's sweet dream,
And say the things that draw me close to thee
Ere slumber close our eyes in still of night?
I hear again thy oft repeated vows.
Would thou wert nigh to still my wavering
   thoughts,
And speak once more the words that are my bliss—
That feed my heart which thou hast hunger taught.

i shall come **to her**

 If some there be with agéd mien
Who wisely smile at love,
And say 'tis but a childish dream
And one they are above,

To them I say who sit and smile,
Because they so prefer,
I pray I shall not die until
My feet have come to her.

I know somewhere tonight she sits
Within her father's home,
While I a foot-loose wanderer
Am destined still to roam.

But I shall find her out I know,
And thus within her place
She calmly sits and waits for me,
And she will know my face.

And one sweet day, we two shall meet,
Whatever may occur;
And so content I wander on,
For I shall come to her.

the loveless

marveled

She had a sorrow once,
Born of bliss;
'Twas but a hand, a voice,
A lover's kiss.

It grew like mountain trees,
Strong and tall.
This sorrow grew to be
Her all in all.

It touched her lips to song.
Over reeds
Her fingers played—her hands
To kindly deeds.

38

The loveless marveled much,
Seeing this;
Not understanding aught
The lover's kiss.

at the
dance

We circled oft the hall in varying motions,
And talked, through all the music wrought,
Of friends and dress and common things;
But here is the speech I thought:

"Before the night has yielded all its music
And the dance is o'er and dawn is here,
And the dream waltz plays as each sleeps on,
Oh, say you love me, dear!

"I hold you near to me; you are my captive;
And the mellow night is full of dew,
And as the winking, sleepy stars
Wink on, I dance with you.

"Oh, say you love me, dear, while yet the music
Still trembles through the waves of night,
Your fallen curls creep o'er my face,
And the house of life is light!

"For o'er and o'er again this evening's dancing
I'll dance with you in memory's hall,
And feel your whispers on my cheek
And the rebel curls that fall.

"And when life's lonely way grows hard and narrow,
And some great lord your hand shall sue,
I'll then remember fondly still
That I have danced with you."

Instead, we talked of friends and dress and
    nothings;
And the silent speech my heart had said
Lay silent still, and the dance wore on,
Till the dance and night were fled.

to-morrow
i'm away

Come here and take my hand

And press my lips,

Just for today—

To-morrow I'm away;

With pulsing heart

And quickened feet

I'll tread another street;

And in the toils

Of duty's net

I may sometimes forget

You for awhile,

And this sweet day

In life's all stormy way;

And oft I'll know

The want of heart

Again life's work to start,

So press my lips

Just for today—

To-morrow I'm away.

love's
paradox

Here is my hand,
It holds my heart,
You understand.

And with it goes
Whate'er may come
Of joys and woes.

It is my all
I give to you
This even's fall.

My hand—take it—
Gently—the heart—
You will break it!

And yet I know
'Twill surely break
If you let go.

43

i give myself **for love**

O you who love me, do you wish to bind
Me fast; when you grow cold
That no escape I find?

My heart I cannot barter for all days,
Though swearing with my tongue
A thousand, thousand ways.

The house of love is spirit, and no key
Will firmly close its doors
Forever and for thee.

Yet if you love but me, the one true way,
Without agreements long,
I'll go with you to-day.

But if by spring or noon of summer you
Look sad upon my face,
We'll smile and say adieu.

Glad, glad that we have tasted to the core
The sweet of all the world,
Though we shall taste no more.

For this I give my all—below, above,
On earth, and after it—
I give myself for love.

he will **come**

He will come, she said
Deep in her bounding, girlish heart, and smiled,
Assurance on her lips;
And childhood's dreaming fancies wild
That over blissful pathways led—
He will come, she said.

He will come, she said,
As many daily tasks and years came on;
And from her cherry lips
And cheeks the girlish glow had gone;
And though her glad, wild dreams had fled—
He will come, she said.

He will come, she said,
As o'er the saddened chords of her pure heart
The hand of bitterness
Oft now and then a tune would start,
When some old playmate's life was wed—
He will come, she said.

He will come, she said,
And sweetly smiled with faith again serene,
In that one perfect love
Beyond the faded and the green
Of earth. Ere last they laid her dead,
He has come, she said.

to you who come
at evening

I know you oft have told me, dear,
The world is full of hate and strife;
But I'm content with you and life—
With you each night beside me here.

You often fear that I am sad,
Because some things you think I miss;
I would not lose a single kiss
For that which makes some persons glad.

And when you touch me with your hand,
And say the words you used to say,
Why—all the night is turned to day,
And I forget the things I'd planned.

And often when we here have sat,
And I have said, "Tell me again,"
I've seen you smile a bit, but then,
You see, we women live on that.

We women love that we may live;
The heart is hungry, too, and I—
No matter if you don't know why—
Well, I'm content with what you give.

the loves
of other years

Where are they,
The loves of other years,
The smiles, the walks in evening still,
The limpid, lithesome, fancy-worlds
With cherished secrets none shall know
Of childish hopes and fears—
Where are they,
The loves of other years?

Where are they?
The loves of other years,
When sunny paths led through the fields,
Oft trod by feet that hastened not,
To cooling, shady woods where dwelt
Sweet endless dreams of life's good cheers—
Where are they,
The loves of other years?

50

Where are they,
The loves of other years,
The eyes of faith, the timid touch
And gentle voice, the dainty step
Across the silvery, singing creek,
The face that ever still appears—
Where are they,
The loves of other years?

Where are they,
The loves of other years,
The lips that sang the nursery songs,
And they that in the noiseless night,
In whispers low and unforgot,
Betrayed their hearts with laughs and tears—
Where are they,
The loves of other years?

Where are they,
The loves of other years—
In some far world of endless bliss,
With sweet caress and hand in hand,
Do they again live as on earth?
O Thou, whose love my question hears,
Where are they,
The loves of other years?

Where are they,
The loves of other years?
Old memory will not let them pass.
Though faded be the pictures now
In dusty bygone galleries old,
Again I ask as evening nears—
Where are they,
The loves of other years?

where love
abides

Where love abides
There is no talk of duties mine and yours;
The ever glowing light within allures
Each willing foot and hand
To move or still to stand
Whate'er betides—
Where love abides.

Where love abides
There is no grief or secret inner thought
Or plan or longing hope the day has wrought
But each may fully know
The purport high or low;
And no one chides
Where love abides.

Where love abides
The first gray gloom of leaden falling dark
Brings joy; and each will hasten and will hark
To hear that sweet old sound,
As footsteps oft resound
At eventides—
Where love abides.

Where love abides
The tender buds of gentleness within
Will bloom the day had stifled 'mid the din;
And solitude grows sweet
Where hands so quickly meet
And lips besides—
Where love abides.

Where love abides
The silvery breaking dawn once more finds mates
United in their secret themes and fates
Forever and a day;
And so runs life away
In goodly strides
Where love abides.

o dream
of love!

Lost in olden dreams and gleeful songs,
I tread again the garden paths of youth.
The joys of myriad hopes in twilight's hour,
And visions in the shadowed starry night,
Lift up my heart unto my parted lips,
Like one whose talent is in song. And as
The kindly earth yields forth each spring
Her budding brood, so in my barren heart
There blooms again the rose of sweet content.
O'er worldly din and godless strife of men
Arise the symphonies of endless peace;
Resurrected is the human heart
From out the grave of withered selfishness,
And touched to song the moistened lips of love.
They awake that slumbered in their gold,
With tender arms enfolding them that want.

Tired men that tread the crowded streets
Find a place of sweet repose at night,
And fill with love the hearts of lonely women.
From myriad mother arms come forth sweet babes,
Like budding roses dewy fresh at dawn,
To light with joy the byways of the earth.—
O dream of love! endure through speeding years
That I shall pass in worldly din and dust,
A shining light to cheer my wand'ring steps,
As long ago in sunlit paths of youth.

a woman's **question**

Am I not meek?
I give my hand, my lips, my cheek,
My dear, to you,
My life, my soul; and shall not rue.

Sink deep in joy
And revel long; I'll be your toy,
My dear. From now
To play the part you'll teach me how.

To your desire
Of dawn and dark, though like the fire,
My dear, I yield,
As withered grass in a burning field.

Your heart's caprice,
For all of me, will it ne'er cease,
My dear, to cling
To both the flesh and soul I bring?

the old **philosopher**

He was nearly seventy. Forty-four years he had lived
  in the same apartment.
He sat looking out of a window, which had a view
  down a street of fashionable residences.
He had known many families of three or four
  generations.
He was thinking, "Always the pattern is the same:
  Young man, young woman, sex, love. Young
  woman's parents anxious their daughter should be
  taken care of; marriage; children.
"Next generation: sons must make money to
  support wives; daughters must get husbands
  to have a home and be taken care of; marriage;
  children.
"Next generation the same.
"And so on and on: love, marriage, children,
  ad infinitum. What's it all for?

"Always the same pattern. But nobody asks,
   What for?"

                *   *   *

Thus mused the old philosopher, as he had often
   done.
His niece came in. She told him she was about
   to be married.
Philosopher: Why?
Niece: But, uncle, I love him!

soul **and body**

Ah yes, dear one, it is our hope to meet
Sometime, somewhere, in some great after-life,
Where senseless fate's cruel lash shall no more beat
Upon our flesh, and gone this world of strife!

But I am joyless in this thought; for where
Will be your tender lips that I have pressed,
Your hand that I have touched, your silken hair,
By morning twilight tangled, dream-caressed?

What joy of spirit-world could pay the loss
Of your dear self so full of honeyed sweet,
Your lovely smile that lightened many a cross?
Such immortality seems incomplete.

forever

The back porch of a cottage a little way out of town.

    It is late. All is still. An elderly man and woman
    sit talking, her head on his shoulder.

HE. It seems strange—all the children gone.

SHE. It was just so when we were first married—
    you and I alone.

HE. That was long ago.

SHE. It seems only a few years.

HE. We passed through some hard times.

SHE. Yes; but we passed through them together.
    I wish we might go on this way forever.

HE. I will wait for you if I go first.

SHE. We will wait for each other.

HE. Think how many men and women, through
    the ages, have made promises like that.

SHE. When I was a little girl I remember once
    hearing my father and mother say something
    like that. I didn't understand them.

63

HE. What if there is nothing after this!

SHE. That would be terrible.

HE. We have had each other here.

SHE. Yes, we have had each other here.

HE. What a night!

SHE. These countless stars!

HE. They seem to promise that there is something else after this, that somewhere we shall be together again.

SHE. You and I going on like this forever.

HE. Forever.